The EYFS Inspection
in practice

by Jenny Barber and Sharon Paul-Smith

Contents

Illustrated by Cathy Hughes

Published by Practical Pre-School Book, A Division of MA Education
St Jude's Church, Dulwich Road, Herne Hill, London, SE24 0PB
Tel: 020 7501 6753 www.practicalpreschoolbooks.com
© 2009 MA Education

The EYFS Inspection in practice ISBN 9781904575856

Introduction

This book is designed to support you in the completion of your SEF and to give suggestions as to how to make the most of your Ofsted inspection. The SEF has received a mixed reception, but this book aims to explain and show its comprehensive value.

The book is set out in clear chapters to guide you through the processes, with checklists and reference charts for you to work through in your setting.

We begin with reflective practice as this is an essential tool for continual development within a setting, both for individuals and the setting as a whole. The skills and awareness that are honed through reflective practice will support both the completion of the SEF and looking at how to develop practice following your inspection.

The chapter on the Self-Evaluation Form has a comprehensive grid, guiding you through each section of the SEF with suggestions and points for consideration to help you complete the SEF relevantly and constructively. These grids provide a much fuller explanation of the questions posed in the Ofsted Early Years Self Evaluation Guidance document. Additionally, there are suggestions for evidence you could make available to back up your statements.

We then move onto other preparations you may make for an inspection and general principles of good practice for all visitors to your setting and the involvement of all practitioners working in the setting. These are explored in 'First Impressions Count' and 'Preparing for your Inspection.' A first impressions checklist will help you to objectively look at your setting and identify how a visitor might see your setting.

The chapter on the "Inspection Day' explores how to cope on the day and support staff as well as the importance of paying close attention to the feedback you receive from the inspector. "After the inspection" looks at how you can take your practice forward and move on, regardless of your grading outcome.

Throughout the book there are case studies of real inspection situations to help illustrate different points for thought and discussion. All in all this book is designed to enable anyone working in the early years, be as a childminder, nursery nurse or reception teacher, to make their EYFS inspection a positive and stress-free experience.

Reflective Practice

In the DfES publication Key Elements for Effective Practice (02/2005), it states that:

"Effective practice in the early years requires committed, enthusiastic and reflective practitioners with a breadth and depth of knowledge, skills and understanding."

For a long time it has been considered good practice for practitioners to reflect on their own practice, it is a phrase widely used, but what does it mean exactly and how should we reflect? There are in fact two terms that you should be familiar with: reflective practice and reflective practitioners.

Reflective Practice

This means thinking about and analysing your actions and practice with a view to changing, developing and improving practice.

Reflective Practitioner

This describes a practitioner who is aware of their strengths and skills and additionally their knowledge gaps and areas for skill development and are ready to work to develop them.

So, it is not just being aware of what you do and what your strengths and skills are, it is about taking action and moving forward. It is about identifying what you could do differently, how you could better support the children and work more effectively with your team.

There are many benefits to reflective practice and being a reflective practitioner.

Benefits for the individual include:

+ Skills are developed

+ More motivated

+ Greater job satisfaction

+ Personal development

+ Become an agent of change

+ Better able to meet the needs of children and their families

+ More confident

+ Able to meet challenges presented within the job role

+ Stronger professional relationships within the team

Benefits for the children:

+ Their individual needs are more likely to be effectively met

+ The learning environment will better meet their needs

+ Practitioners have a greater understanding of how to support their development

Benefits for the setting:

+ A more effective setting with highly skilled and motivated staff

+ Staff feel more valued

+ Children are happy and settled as their needs are met and supported, leading to happy parents and a good reputation for the setting

+ More organised and efficient

+ Staff become agents of change and ensure that the setting is constantly evolving and developing

+ Setting is perceived to be innovative with a focussed vision

So the benefits may well be numerous, but how do you start to be a reflective practitioner? For purposeful and effective reflective practice, we need to invest time in the process, so that it becomes part of everyone's way of working.

Most people are already doing it without realising it. The observations we carry out, the reflection on children's needs and interests and how we use that information to inform planning are all partial reflections, and the skills honed through that practice can help us to be good 'reflectors'.

We need to begin though with ourselves and the need to be completely truthful. Reflective practice is never going to be truly effective unless we are 100% honest with ourselves about what we do, remembering there is a distinct difference between what we might say or think we do and what we actually do. Reflection is like putting a mirror up to your work and seeing from the reverse viewpoint what you are doing.

Some practitioners may need additional support to look clearly into the mirror, and identify what it is they say they do and what they actually do. This necessary support will largely depend on their learning style and ability to objectively analyse.

Let's begin with some straightforward basic questions about ourselves as positive role models and then move on to our knowledge, awareness and understanding of individual key children.

Reflect on your practice in relation to these questions about being a positive role model, remembering to be honest and truthful:

+ I always say hello and good morning to the people around me.

+ I offer to help other staff members set up or tidy away.

My Inspection Case Study

Children in the setting were asked individually what it was like to be a child in the setting. When asked if they knew all the adults in the setting one child reported that he didn't know the lady in the red cardigan who has a clipboard. This lady is an NVQ assessor and visits the setting frequently. This comment led us to reflect on and improve the fact that we don't always take the trouble to fully introduce visitors to the children, as this comment came from an older child, we are very aware that younger children may find it even more confusing.

Room Leader of a Pre-School in a Day Nursery

+ I always say please and thank you.

+ I am patient.

+ I like to help people.

+ I listen to other people's points of view.

+ I am tidy and organised.

Having done that, you can then move on to thinking about a specific child. Your perception might be, as with the questions above, that you do that all the time, but do you? Choosing one of your key children, ask the following questions:

How often do you smile and acknowledge the child positively?

How much time do you spend listening to and talking to the child?

What type of activities does the child enjoy most?

How do you use these activities to help the child learn?

The following questions are more challenging and are ask you to reflect more deeply. It would be interesting to do a comparison between two of your key children, one you feel you know well and another you feel you don't know so well.

Having eased yourself in, you can then begin to delve into specific aspects of your work using the following techniques to help you gain an insight.

+ To begin you need to question what you do, why you do it and how you do it and then think about your thoughts and responses. This might be done individually or as a team.

+ Could it be done differently: are there alternatives that could be better or more effective? Ask 'what if?' Test new ideas, maybe visit other settings to gain a different insight and perspective.

+ Remember to be open-minded: don't just assume a new way of doing something won't work, have a go and see what happens, you might be surprised.

+ As you seek alternatives consider the different points of views of those involved/affected e.g. parents, children, other staff.

+ Use reflective practice to identify and resolve problems, using a problem solving approach.

There are many aspects of practice that can be considered e.g. partnership with parents, snack time, management of behaviour, hygiene routines, child initiated opportunities in the outside environment. The principles into practice cards in the EYFS pack provide a good selection of tools for reflective practice.

EYFS Themes

EYFS Theme: a unique child – keeping safe

What activities or experiences in the setting help children to think about:

+ the things that make them feel good about themselves?

+ the people who help them?

+ how to keep themselves safe?

+ how to recognise and avoid possible danger?

+ reasons for making particular choices?

+ the reason they are allowed to do or to have some things and not other things?

EYFS Theme: enabling environments - the learning environment

+ How well do you reflect examples of outdoor learning in your observations and assessments of children?

+ Does indoor provision meet the needs of all the children as both a place to feel at home and a place to learn?

+ How do you ensure that the deployment of staff is flexible enough to respond to the flow and movement of children between indoors and outdoors?

EYFS Theme: learning and development - creativity and critical thinking

+ What open–ended activities do you provide for children in your setting?

+ Do you give children the experience of playing with paint and glue before expecting them to use them to make a Christmas card?

+ Have you ever taped your interactions with children to see how you support the development of creativity and critical thinking?

To gain a clearer insight into specific aspects of practice, you could work through the questions outlined in photocopiable sheets at the end of this chapter or refer to the text boxes with lists of questions.

Supporting Your Team

+ How do you ensure that team members understand their roles and responsibilities?

+ How do you support members of the team in their work?

+ Do you actively recognise an individual's strengths?

+ How often do you provide feedback on staff performance?

+ How do you ensure that their work is interesting and valuable?

+ Do you encourage team members to take on responsibility?

+ How do you ensure that team members are able to extend their knowledge, skills and experience?

+ Do you act upon things that have been said to you, are you seen as being pro-active?

+ What opportunities have you provided for staff to contribute new ideas and develop their capabilities?

It isn't sufficient to simply ask the questions and reflect on your practice: you then have to take action to develop practice and move forward. You need to identify how this can be done, who will need to be involved and whether any additional support or training will be required.

Keeping records of discussions on reflective practice and documenting how you are going to move forward, shows good practice in relation to self assessment.

This can be done in two ways, depending on whether this relates to the individual or for the team or setting as a whole. Records kept as part of the appraisal and supervision process will show how the individual is

a reflective practitioner. For the team or setting as a whole, the easiest way to do this is to complete an action plan, identifying what you need to develop in terms of practice. The targets set in the action plan must be **SMART**:

Specific – clearly identified as actions

Measurable – it must clearly show it can be seen that the actions have been achieved or not

Achievable – practitioners can work easily to achieve them

Realistic – all the necessary tools need to be available so the actions can be achieved

Time bound – a date identified when the actions need to be achieved by or identifying when there will be a review

The photocopiable sheet at the end of the chapter shows a reflective practice action plan.

Failing to act upon what has been identified through reflective practice can have a demotivating effect, so the follow through action is essential. This is particularly important for managers supporting practitioners in the setting.

As practitioners become more aware and reflective practice skills are developed, they may wish to keep a reflective practice diary. This type of diary can be a record of what is useful

to you and a memory cue. It may describe significant incidents relating to practice and facilitate evaluation of these incidents and implications for practice.

Becoming a reflective practitioner as previously stated gives a much clearer insight into a individual's role, and once this insight has evolved, more searching questions can be asked.

+ How do I see my role?

+ What kind of practitioner do I think I am: what are my key skills and strengths?

+ What are my personal thoughts on the role of early years education?

+ How do I show that I am consistent at all times in my practice?

Once reflective practice becomes integral to what happens within the setting, the benefits will quickly become clear, and practitioners will as a result be committed to achieving high standards in all aspects of practice.

Reflective Practice Questions

SUPPORTING CHILDREN'S PLAY

How do you encourage children to be active in their play and learning?

How do you identify additional resources to enhance play as part of continuous provision?

When do you stand back from children's play?

When do you join in with children's play?

How do you support children to take responsibility for developing their own play?

SUPPORTING CHILDREN'S LEARNING

Do you feel the children were absorbed and interested in the activity?

Can you identify what it was that helped children to be interested and involved in the experience?

Were children encouraged to take control and be actively involved in their learning during the activity?

How did you encourage children to be active in their play and learning?

What do you feel the children learnt from the activity? How did it support their development?

Was this learning planned or spontaneous?

How could this learning be reinforced or built upon?

What types of resources were used and were there enough resources?

How did the children use the resources?

What further resources could have been used?

Were there any limitations to this activity?

Did the children extend the learning opportunity through the use of new resources or ideas?

The Self-Evaluation Form

So, why is there now so much emphasis on the Self-Evaluation Form (SEF)? Research has proven that self-reflection and evaluation both support good practice within a setting as part of continual development. Importantly this self-reflection supports good outcomes for children.

The EPPE (Effective Provision of Pre-School Education) project was very influential in informing us of the significance of self-reflection and evaluation.

"The use of self evaluation...should enable settings to reflect on their current strengths and identify next steps which will have a direct impact on children's learning experiences."

In their efforts to continually improve outcomes for children, Ofsted decided to implement a specific early years self-evaluation tool.

Although the completion of the Self-Evaluation Form is not compulsory, all settings are advised to complete the form. Both completion of the form and failure to complete the form can have a very significant effect on the outcome of your inspection.

+ If you do complete your SEF, it is likely to decrease the length of the inspection and helps the inspector to know what to focus on in the inspection. If completed properly the SEF can ease the process of inspecting for the inspector.

+ If you do not complete your SEF, you will more than likely be asked why and will need a good reason as to why it has not be completed.

+ Failure to complete the form could also mean that your inspection will be longer and more searching. The self-evaluation criteria is likely to be graded lower, although the inspector will check to see what other methods of self-evaluation have been implemented.

Before tackling the SEF, it is worth spending some time reflecting on your setting and its current self-assessment strategies. Settings where reflective practice occurs regularly will find completion of the SEF a much easier task. For further tips on becoming a reflective practitioner please see the previous chapter.

Managers and leaders in settings need to consider what is already being done in the setting to evaluate quality and practice, and how good practice is shared throughout the setting.

The basic key questions of self-evaluation are:

+ How are we doing?

+ How do we know?

+ What are we going to do now?

Involving all staff in the process of self-evaluation will produce higher standards and a sense of ownership over the process of continual development. It is worth remembering that self evaluation only works where individuals within a setting are committed to ensuring high standards and are able to look objectively at practice.

All practitioners need to be aware of what the priorities for improvement are as identified in the SEF, and their role in the ongoing process of working towards improvement. As the SEF is a working document which plays an important role in the development of the setting, please bear in mind that Ofsted will look to validate the statements in your SEF by questioning all staff, whether they are new-starters or not. It is essential then that the settings's SEF is included in the induction process so that all new members of staff are aware of how the setting sees itself.

Using reflective practice as part of your self-assessment process within the setting will greatly help and support completion of the Self-Evaluation Form. When you first look at the SEF it may look a daunting task to complete it, but break it down section by section and setting yourself small completion steps can make it seem much more manageable.

The Self-Evaluation Form – what you need to know

Practicalities

+ The SEF can be completed on-line and Ofsted recommend that you use this method.

+ You can update your SEF on-line as often as you like, probably termly but it should be updated no less than once a year.

My Inspection Case Study

Each room in the nursery was asked to take a blank SEF, and fill in information that they felt was relevant to their room. The nursery management then pulled all the information together from each room and with input from head office then completed the SEF. This proved to be an easy way to ensure that all staff were involved in the process. Moving ahead the nursery has created a committee of parent representatives and the parents are now also asked to provide information for the SEF.

Nursery Manager, Teddies Nursery, Twickenham West

My Inspection Case Study

A leader in a setting commented that the first time she and her staff completed the SEF it was a very lengthy and time-consuming process. She acknowledged though that once the form had been filled out first time round, it would never take so long again to modify and update.

Pre-School Leader

- An annually updated hard copy needs to be sent to Ofsted.

- You need a copy of the SEF in the setting at all times ready for the inspector.

- To complete the online form you will need an Ofsted Security Token (OST), which is a unique password, and the guidelines on how to complete the online form. If you have not received an OST you need to contact Ofsted (08456 404043) quoting your Unique Reference Number.

HINT: Around two days before your inspection, your on-line SEF will most likely be frozen. This will give you a warning that the inspector is on their way!

Tips for completing the SEF

- Start with the section you find easiest to complete to give yourself a boost, then progress gradually to completing all of the form.

- Make your statements clear and concise and add evidence to back up your statements e.g. refer to policies, planning, observations, records etc., and have these to hand for the inspector to review.

- Use bullet points rather than lengthy paragraphs.

- Try and convey as full a picture as possible of your setting.

- Use a dictionary if you're unsure of a correct spelling. To use a spell check you will need to cut and paste into a word document, as there is no spell check with the on-line form.

- Ensure you use appropriate terminology and language and avoid jargon and slang.

- Use the Ofsted guidance notes.

- Even though will be graded separately, it is important to reinforce it throughout the whole SEF.

How to grade yourself

- Be honest, if you feel your provision and/or practice in a specific area is outstanding say so and why.

- Even if you grade yourself as outstanding, you still need to identify areas for improvement and what you are hoping to do to make it even better.

- Ofsted will look at how their judgment compares to yours and in doing so will be evaluating your judgements and ability to self evaluate.

The self-evaluation form is broken down into three parts. These parts are:

Part A

This part covers the setting details and views of those who use the setting. This details the characteristics of your setting and the background of the children. It also asks you to seek the views of all those who use your setting and how you use these views to improve the quality of the provision.

Part B

Evaluation of the outcomes for children, this should help you think about and assess your provision. You should answer the questions by taking account of the welfare, learning and development requirements and statutory guidance set out in the EYFS framework.

You should think carefully about any changes and improvements you have made since your most recent inspection. In the text boxes you should describe briefly what you think is working best and describe any plans you have to further improve provision.

Tell Ofsted about any evidence you have that supports what you are saying e.g. photographs, documents, risk assessment. These should then be available for the inspector when they visit.

Part C

This is were you supply information about how you meet the statutory requirements of the EYFS framework and where you can state if you are registered on either or both parts of the Childcare Register.

My Inspection Case Study

A group of practitioners from different settings were discussing the SEF. One practitioner said she felt that by completing the SEF they were being asked to do Ofsted's job for them. Another practitioner disagreed, saying she felt the SEF gave her an opportunity to show everything that was done well in her setting, and take a sense of pride in good practice and achievements. This was supported by another practitioner, who stated that Ofsted only gain a snapshot of a setting during an inspection, but the SEF gives them a much broader and fuller picture of the setting as a whole.

Practitioners from a mixture of settings

My Inspection Case Study

I had set a target to complete my SEF by the end of the month, but my inspection happened before then. I had completed about three quarters of my SEF, as I had run out of time. To complete my SEF I reread my policies and reflected on my practice and implementation of the EYFS.

The inspector stayed with me for 4 hours and said she would not have been here so long if my SEF had been fully completed. The inspector was lovely and very friendly. I was asked many questions and there was some cross questioning to build up a picture of how I was meeting the EYFS. Despite being apprehensive, I felt prepared for the inspection and was pleased with the outcome.

Sarah Cann, Childminder, Buckinghamshire.

Step-by-step guide to completing your Self-evaluation Form

Part A: Section 1 - Your setting

This is the only section of the SEF that Ofsted can quote verbatim in the report – be sure it is factual and to the point.

You need to state the number of children who use the setting and give a brief description of their ages, genders, social and cultural backgrounds and whether they have learning difficulties and special educational needs.

Here you can list any special features of your setting e.g. participation in a quality assurance scheme.

Questions from page 8 of the Ofsted SEF guidance	Features to consider
Your building including area and rooms used	• Describe your building – its age and style. • List any other users.
The area your provision is in	• Is it a residential or industrial area, rural or urban?
Any access to an outdoor space	• Do you have an outdoor area that children can use on a daily, free-flow basis? • If not what access to outdoor play do you have?
Access to and within the building – such as a lift, ramp or stairs	• Describe access and give consideration to access for those with additional needs. This must include plans for what you would do should a need arise.
The days and hours you operate	
The number and qualifications of the adults working with the children and any support staff such as a cook	• List qualifications of all staff – check with current legislation that levels and percentages are correct.
Recent training attended or any qualifications gained	• List training taken within the past year including any relevant short courses
Difficulties in recruiting and retaining staff	• Describe any problems you may have had in this area
Recent or impending re-organisation or change of staff	• Is anyone about to leave or to become qualified? • Is there any impending internal promotion?

Part A: Section 2 – Views of those who use your setting

Questions from page 8 of the Ofsted SEF guidance	Features to consider/ reflective questions	Evidence suggestions
How do you know what their views are	• Did you issue a questionnaire to ask parents their views? • Are parents provided with open-door access to the setting and an opportunity to air their views?	How did you use the information gained from responses to your questionnaire? Have you got examples of changes made as a result? Do you have a summary sheet of key responses?
Do you ask parents and others to complete a questionnaire about how satisfied they are with the provision or do you meet with parents to discuss the provision?	• Do you have a questionnaire for new parents as part of the settling in process? Do you give out the questionnaire annually as well as an exit questionnaire?	As above – do you have evidence of dates and times of such meetings and copies of questionnaires? Do you have a summary of responses to questionnaires?
Are parents represented on the management body?	• Refer to a parents group or a pre-school committee	
How do you know children's views and ideas and those of the staff?	• Do you do a review of each session with the children? • Do you regularly ask children for their views and ideas of what they would like to do with the provision? • Are staff able to express their ideas freely and are these ideas embraced if practically possible? • Do you have staff interviews and appraisals to consider their views and ideas?	Children could be given cameras and asked to take photographs of areas they like or dislike about the setting such as outdoor space. What changes have you made in response to those views – show evidence e.g. in the form of an action plan.

Part A: Section 3 - The learning and development of the children in the early years provision.

The table below will help you to consider the questions on page 10 and 11 of the SEF guidance booklet. Links can be made to the Early Years Foundation Stage card 4.4: Areas of Learning and Development. You must be able to show academic progress.

Questions from pages 10 and 11 of the SEF guidance	Features to consider	Evidence suggestions
What is your overall approach to the children's learning and development?	• Is your planning child centred? • Are children able to make choices? • Can children lead activities? • What is the proportion of child initiated and adult-led activities?	Provide copies of plans annotated with responses to children's interests, link these plans to your observations. Children's choices must go beyond the choice of whether to participate in an activity or not.
How do you know that what you do helps children?	• Do you have a system of observing and then evaluating observations of every child?	Copies of observations using a variety of observation methods detailing every child's individual learning journey.
How do you know that children are making progress towards the early learning goals?	• How do you ensure that each child accesses all areas of learning? • Do you make regular observations in all areas of learning? • Is there a strategy to ensure you are working towards goals logically and using the development matters descriptors as a guide?	Copies of observations indicating what next steps are required for the child – these need to be carried forward to note when next steps are tried and the results.

What works well? What could be improved?	• A clear description of what works well and why you think that is. • What you feel could be developed and improved, with an approximate time scale.	
Does planning and assessment link to children's individual achievements?	• Are plans annotated to show responses to children's needs? • How do you plan to meet individual children's achievements?	Can you show evidence that you use the planning cycle?
What are children doing to show that your planning and the adult interaction is helping them to enjoy and achieve?	• This is about progression, how children use the resources and what they like to use. It concerns their responses to the environment and to adults.	Photographs could depict children having fun in the setting or of celebrating their achievements.

How well do you and any assistants of staff who work with you do the following:

Questions from pages 10 and 11 Ofsted SEF guidance	Features to consider	Evidence suggestions
Support learning in your interactions with children	• Do you and your staff ask open-ended questions? (Questions that require more than a yes or no answer.) • Do staff give children a chance to think before they speak, and listen to their responses? • Are staff good role models? • Do they support children's vocabulary? • Do staff scaffold children to the next level?	When scaffolding, do staff know when to stand back? You could use photographic evidence. Tape recordings. MP3 players or observations. Do you provide opportunities for sustained shared thinking?
Plan the learning environment to help children progress towards the early learning goals	• Do you adjust continuous provision to reflect individual needs? • Do you plan the environment in a way that children can access all areas of learning and are these areas of learning clearly defined? • Are all areas of learning covered in each session, both indoors and outdoors?	Use plans of resources and activities provided with photographic evidence.
Plan children's play and exploration in and out of doors with a balance of adult-led and child-led activities that helps children to think critically and be active and creative learners	• Do children have choice? • Do you allow uninterrupted free-flow play? • Do you use open-ended resources? • How do you demonstrate to children that the end product may not always be important? • How do you support children in making connections between experiences?	Open-ended resources are those that have no specific purposes e.g. boxes, leaves, lengths of material, these things and others allow critical thinking and problem solving.
Plan for individual children	• Do you have an Inclusion Officer? • Does your Inclusion Officer attend all relevant meetings and training and then cascade information? • Do you meet the needs of all children including different learning styles? • How do you ensure continuity of care? • Do you liaise with outside agencies?	

Use information from observation and assessment	• This is about using the planning cycle, refer to previous answer.	
Identify and provide for additional learning and development needs including those children who achieve beyond what is expected	• What provision do you have for these children? • How do you identify these children?	This is simply meeting individual needs. You need to think about how you identify these children i.e. assessments.
Involve parents and carers as partners and other agencies and providers in children's learning and development	• How do you involve parents in the work of the setting? • Do you have parent consultation meetings at a time and place • Convenient to parents and carers? • Do parents contribute to policies, observations and children's records?	Research shows that if parents are engaged in early years provision they will remain so throughout their child's education – however we must respect that some parents do not want to be so involved. What do you do to embrace all parents e.g. home visits, translating documents and sending out letters. Do you have a policy of the month for parents and staff to comment on and show examples of changes made in response to this. Do you include parents' observations of their children in the children's records?
Offer an inclusive and welcoming service to all children	• Refer to questions on card 2.2 EYFS - Do you display lists from home languages? • Find out from parents the greetings that they use – encourage parents and staff to use these greetings. • Make sure that everyone: parent, carer, sibling etc receives a warm welcome.	Consider your welcome routine – could this be improved? Does the key person welcome all of their key children? Remember that this should also take into account individual needs and learning styles. Make sure you reflect positive images.

Section 4: The welfare of the children in the early years provision.

These questions are taken from the Every Child Matters Agenda with the addition of the question, eg, how effectively is the welfare of children in the EYFS promoted?

Questions from page 11 Ofsted SEF guidance	Features to consider	Evidence suggestions
How well do you and staff take steps to ensure the key people safeguard and promote the welfare of the children	• Do you have a key person system with someone to cover should that key person not be available? • Do the children know who their key person is? • Does the key person keep records of children confidential?	Are there photos of key people and lists of their children. Do key people greet their children and spend time with them each session and form a special relationship with carers of their key children and liaise with other providers
Promote health and well-being and whether necessary steps are taken to prevent the spread of infection and appropriate action taken when children are ill	• Consent from parents to transport their children to hospital in case of emergency? • What is your medicine policy? • What hygiene routines do you have? • Do you talk to children about the spread of infection and how to reduce this? • You should have up-to-date information from parents or carers of child's medical conditions, allergies, special diet etc.	Copies of consent forms Do staff carry anti-bacterial handwash for use after nose blowing?
Teach children about keeping safe	• Do you teach about the dangers of talking to strangers and their right to protect their own bodies? • Do you provide both safe risks and risk versus challenge?	Demonstrate what safe risks you have in your setting e.g. by surrounding climbing frames with safety mats. Demonstrate risk versus challenge in action by close observation of children to make sure that safety is maintained, without hovering over the child and impending their desire to have a go at things.
Encourage children to develop the habits and behaviours appropriate to good learners, their own needs and the needs of others	• Do you teach children about self-control? • What strategies do you use to promote positive behaviour?	
Ensure the suitability and safety of outdoor and indoor spaces, furniture, equipment and toys	• Do you carry out effective safety checks at the beginning and end of each session and are these evaluated and problems acted upon? • Do you use only Kite marked equipment and toys from a reputable supplier? • Do you have up-to-date insurance?	A copy of hazard and safety checks with changes implemented because of them. A copy of your insurance policy and a public liability certificate.

Helping children to stay safe

Questions from page 12 Ofsted SEF guidance	Features to consider/questions to ask yourself	Evidence suggestions
1. How well do you build on children's individual knowledge and ability to identify safety issues and teach children to: • Behave in ways that are safe for themselves and for others • Develop an understanding of dangers and how to stay safe	• Do you explain dangers to children and rules and boundaries in a way that they can understand? • Do you practice road safety with the children? • Do you use opportunities in the routine and play to discuss danger and keeping safe? • How do you balance risk versus challenge? For examples how do you ensure that the children are challenged and allowed to have a go whilst maintaining safety at all times? Do you allow children to assess risks for themselves? • Fire and evacuation drills? Is there a named person in charge of these? • Do you only release children to a named carer – are children aware of this? • Do you have a sun protection policy and do you support children to understand the need for sun protection? • Do you ask the children if they feel safe in the setting?	Posters next to equipment which say, for example, that four people may play on this at one time. Do you have photographic evidence of children using the road safety equipment? Books that explore safety issues. A copy of your sun protection policy – this should state intent to involve all children in its implementation
2. How well you help children from different ethnic backgrounds, any children with learning difficulties and those learning English as an additional language to stay safe	• This question is a common thread throughout the whole of this section – you need to consider it when answering every part. • Do you use practical examples for staying safe so that language is not a barrier? • How do you make children aware of how to do a fire drill if they have receptive language delay, for example? • Are staff aware of cultural practices that may affect safety?	Pictorial Posters Photos of practical examples – e.g. role play Helping Children to be healthy

Helping Children to be healthy

Questions from page 12 Ofsted SEF guidance	Features to consider/questions to ask yourself	Evidence suggestions
1. How well you teach children to: • Be active and understand the benefits of physical activity • Understand and adopt healthy habits • Make healthy choices about what to eat and drink	• Do you have a healthy eating policy? • What training have staff had? • Is water available at all times and are children encouraged to drink especially in hot weather – can young children reach their drink? • Do children have the choice to rest and to be active? • Do children have the opportunity to make choices about what they eat, including food from a variety of cultures? • Does each child have their own flannel, bed linen and hairbrush if these are used? • There should be a separate toilet and hand basin for every ten children over two years. This does not apply to child minders.	A copy of your healthy eating policy. This is about more than only having fruit at snack time, it is about giving children healthy options and informed choices for a balanced diet and including foods from other cultures. Menu Pictorial instructions for hand washing and nose blowing etc. A copy of food hygiene certificates. Named person responsible for health and safety.
2. How well you take account of children's individual dietary and medical needs	• Do you have an up-to-date medicine policy • Would all adults and children know which children have allergies? • Are staff aware of quarantine periods and symptoms of common childhood illnesses • Do you have a supportive staff sickness policy?	Copy of policy Posters naming children with allergies - a photo of the child is helpful as a volunteer may not know names – names should be withheld from copies shown. These should be removed from the setting if it is being used by other users to protect confidentiality.
2. As question 2 in staying safe, but with regard to being healthy	• Are you good role models? • Are you aware of cultural practice that may affect being healthy.	Copy of training certificate

How well do children enjoy and achieve?

Questions from page 12 Ofsted SEF guidance	Features to consider	Evidence suggestions
1. How well you teach children to: • Make progress towards the early learning goals in relation to their starting points, capabilities and interests. • Be active learners, creative and think critically about what they do. • Work independently and with each other. • Enjoy and have positive attitude towards their learning, to be motivated and keen to learn and communicate their learning. • Have good relationships with other children and take into account each other's diverse needs and backgrounds.	• Are you aware at what stage a child is at when they start at your setting? This can be gathered through liaison with parents and previous providers as well as your own observations after allowing the child time to settle. • How do you support the children's individual learning journey and how do you take into account children's individual interests? • Do you offer a range of experiences that encourage independence and co-operation? • Are activities presented in an exciting way motivating children to want to take part in them? • Do you encourage positive dispositions and attitudes (refer to EYFS card 2.1 and 2.3)?	Do you have evidence of discussions with parents. Records from previous settings. A log of telephone calls to previous providers. Games that need more than one player-opportunities to take turns. Photographs of activities. Describe how you teach children to respect each other in all situations – for example do you use role modelling, role play, story time? Do you draw up a contract of ground rules with the children?

Helping children to make a positive contribution

Questions from page 13 Ofsted SEF guidance	Features to consider	Evidence suggestions
How effectively you encourage children to: • Develop the habits and behaviour appropriate to good learners, their own needs and the needs of others • Join in, make friends, respect each other and take account of each other's diverse needs and backgrounds • Respond to the expectations of others • Make choices and decisions	• Do you create an atmosphere and an environment where children will want to learn and be able to engage and concentrate? Do you provide activities that arouse curiosity and anticipation? • Are children encouraged by good example to value what others say – e.g. being quiet whilst others are speaking. • Are you positive and good role models – are adults within the team friendly towards each other? • Do you use discussion, puppets and story time to help children understand the qualities of friendship and do you encourage the language of friendship? • Do you help children resolve their differences with empathy and sensitivity? • Can children sometimes choose who they sit next to e.g. for snack or lunch time?	
How do you ensure children from different ethnic backgrounds, any children with learning difficulties and or disabilities, and those learning English as an additional language make a positive contribution	• This familiar question underlines every area and needs to be considered carefully to ensure you are supporting all children to make a positive contribution.	
How you ensure that the environment and resources available are accessible to all children	• Do you look at things from a child's perspective eg. are display boards child height , are tables and chairs child sized? • Clearly labelled resources and defined areas. • Are staff deployed in such a way that children can choose indoor or outdoor play?	Photos that children have taken with cameras of how they view things.

Helping children to develop skills for the future.

Questions from Ofsted SEF guidance	Features to consider	Evidence suggestions
Consider carefully how effectively you help children to: • Make as much progress as they can in communicating, literacy, numeracy, and information technology • Develop good habits as active, inquisitive independent learners • Develop collaborative skills – working together, problem solving and creative/ critical thinking • Understand the wider world through their play and communications • Respect each other as individuals, considering culture, ethnicity, background, gender, religion, learning difficulties and/or disabilities	• This section could be linked to the 16 commitments in the EYFS – give examples of opportunities in your setting. • Think about the opportunities you provide that support children to develop these skills e.g treasure baskets, mark making skills, large-scale construction. • Activities that allow for active learning giving children opportunity to explore, experiment and investigate.	Photographs of celebrations and activities set out in appealing ways. Planning. Give examples and strategies of how you meet the needs of children with learning difficulties. Do you share resources with other settings, or borrow resources from a multi-cultural centre?
How well you help children from different ethnic backgrounds and children with learning difficulties and/or disabilities and those learning English as an additional language to develop skills in the future	• Refer to page 41 of the Statutory Framework for the EYFS – this discusses how parents have the choice to send their children to a setting where English is not the first language. Do you have a good relationship with your early years Inclusion team to identify and support such children?	Copies of Individual Learning Plans. Staff training matrix.

Section 5: The leadership and management of the early years provision.

You may not have in place all these recommendations but do mention those that you have implemented, the positive effect they have and those you intend to implement soon.

Questions from page 14 Ofsted SEF guidance	Features to consider/reflective practice	Evidence suggestions
Use self-evaluation to promote improvement	• Does the leader/manager evaluate staff self- assessments to support improvement action plans? • Do you have in-house training and workshops? • Does training address the needs rather than the wants of staff? • Do you have an appraisal system that identifies areas for improvement with follow-up supervision meetings? • Do you have a peer observation system? • Do you plan to allow time for observations of children and staff?	Copies of staff reflective diaries Copies of training plans Copies of staff appraisal and review forms and plans for forthcoming appraisals. Peer observation forms completed and reviewed.
Work in partnership with parents and others	• Is there an open door policy whereby parents can easily approach staff? • Do you have a policy and procedure to support parents with the transitions of their children? • Are All About Me forms completed with the key person, parents and children? • Are parents made aware of your policies and procedures? If so how? Do parents have the opportunity to be involved in the writing of policies? • How do you liaise with other providers, other professionals who may work with a child and schools to ease transitions and inform parents?	A witness statement from a parent. All About Me forms.
Safeguard children	• It is a recommendation that the Criminal Record Bureau (CRB) check is reviewed at least every three years. • Are all staff CRB checked? • You must be prepared for the intended introduction of the vetting and barring scheme due to come into force from Autumn 2009.	CRB certificates. Training matrix indicating which staff require updates and when etc.

How effective is your setting's self evaluation, including the steps taken to promote improvement?

Questions from page 14 Ofsted SEF guidance	Features to consider	Evidence suggestions
The extent to which any recommendations and actions raised at the previous inspection have been tackled in terms of improved outcomes for children	• Do you have an action plan from the last inspection? • Have you exceeded the action plan if so how?	Explain how the action plan worked and any difficulties and barriers that you encountered and how these were overcome.
Any improvements you have made to promote the equality and inclusion that have had a beneficial impact on all children.	• This needs to include specific examples e.g. have you purchased any equipment or books that support inclusion?	Photographs. Written evidence – e.g. a letter from parents
The extent to which improvements have had a positive impact on the overall quality of the service you provide and the outcomes for children.	• Describe the positive impact of change. • Did you have SMART (Specific, Measurable, Achievable, Realistic and Time-bound) targets?	

How well does your setting work in partnership with parents and others?

Questions from pages 14 and 15 of the Ofsted SEF guidance	Features to consider and reflective practice	Evidence suggestions
How effectively do you provide parents and carers with good quality information about the early years provision?	• Do the parents in your setting know how to recognise good provision: do you advise them what to look for? • Do you give parents information about settings other than your own? • Is information accessible to all parents e.g. those with additional needs or those who cannot read? • Do you write regular newsletters etc?	Prospectus Translated newsletters etc
Inform parents and carers about their children's achievements and progress	• Do you have regular consultation meetings? • Do you complete daily or weekly home setting diaries? • Do you give parents free access to observations on their children? • Are you welcoming, accommodating and friendly to parents when they enquire about their children's progress? • Do you take photographs regularly of children? • Do you record children's development for language on an mp3 player or similar and compare to later development to share with parents?	Dates and times of consultation meetings. Parents comments about consultations. Copy of diaries. Witness statement from parents. Photographs MP3 recordings.
Encourage parents and carers to share what they know about their child particularly when the child first starts to attend	• Do you put equal value on observations given to you by parents/carer as to those done by staff?	Copies of All About Me forms
Encourage parents and carers to be involved in supporting children's learning and development	• Do you give parents ideas on how to extend activities and interests at home that have begun in the setting? • Do you hold workshops for parents and carers to understand child development? • Do you explain to parents/carers the stage of development a child is at? • Do you enable children to have schemas and support parents in understanding these? • Do you hold functions such as sports days etc at times when people are likely to be able to attend - e.g. those who work? • Do you make home visits to parents/carers who find it difficult to get to the setting? • Do you use parent work parties to do projects in the setting – for example if you were improving your outdoor provision would you encourage a group of parents and carers to carry out and organise the manual labour or to plan the layout?	Programmes of workshops. Copies of newsletters.

Liaise with external agencies or services with the parents to ensure a child gets the support they need	• You can detail specific examples here. This is about supporting the parents through referrals etc and working together consistently to meet actions set by other professionals and support the child.	Witness statement from parents – all documentation from other agencies.
Liaise with other providers delivering the EYFS for a child or a group of children to ensure progression and continuity of learning and care	• Do you make a record of all telephone calls etc? • Do you use guidance from other settings in providing for children? • Do you liaise with other settings regarding planning?	If you have tried but have been met with a brick wall, evidence would be a record of failed attempts. Records of calls to other providers.

How well do you safeguard all children?

Questions from page 15 Ofsted SEF guidance	Features to consider and reflective practice	Evidence suggestions
The following questions go much deeper and further than having CRB checks and keeping children safe. How well do you help children stay safe?	• Do you explain safety rules to children in a way which they can understand and involve them in drawing up a contract of ground rules? • Do you practice safety routines regularly recording and evaluating their outcomes? • Do you have effective systems to ensure that ratios are kept at all times not only throughout the setting but in individual rooms Do you ensure that all equipment is safe and regularly check this? • Do you evaluate your accident and incident book to consider if there are improvements that you can make to lessen these? • Do you build up good relationships with parents and carers so that concerns can be addressed from a standpoint of mutual trust? • Do all staff and parents and children realise that they have a responsibility to report issues of concern regarding safety? • Is your provision used for your sole use during session time? • Do you have a named officer responsible for health and safety?	Evaluation of safety check forms. A copy of health and safety policy. Ground rules contract.
How well do you ensure the suitability and qualifications of all adults looking after children or having unsupervised access to them	• Do you take up references of all candidates for vacancies? • Do you plan and record continued professional development for all staff according to need? • Do you look at certificates to validate claims of qualifications? • Do you liaise with tutors of qualification courses to see how staff are doing? • Do you support staff when they give you information and ideas from courses?	Copies of advertisements for vacancies. Records of success.
How well you maintain all records that are required for safe and efficient management of the setting and to meet all children's needs	• Where do you keep records? • How do you ensure confidentiality and who has access to records? • When do you record? • How do you ensure data protection on records kept on computers and outside the setting?	Copy of data protection details. It is important to make sure that records are kept on-site or at least are always there when the setting is running unless you have a prior arrangement with Ofsted. You need to check with Ofsted the records that need to be kept on-site.
The effectiveness of your policies and procedures including your complaints procedures	• Do you review policies regularly, allowing parents and staff to contribute in the review? • Do you have many complaints? If not is this an indication that things are working well or are people too afraid to comment?	A copy of policies. Give examples of changes made to policies as a result of a review.

How well you ensure the suitability and safety of outdoor and indoor spaces furniture equipment and toys	• Do you take out annual risk assessments and daily safety checks? • Do you buy appropriate equipment which is quality assured and have available suitable equipment for the age/stage of development of children using it? • Do you have someone responsible for maintenance of equipment?	Copies of daily safety checks with actions taken.
The quality and effectiveness of risk assessments and actions you take to manage or eliminate risks	• Do you analyse incidents and accidents to see if there are adjustments that can be made to lessen the likelihood of accidents happening? • Reviewing risk assessments	Record of accident books and incident books with records of actions taken to ensure less risk in the future. Copies of risk assessment forms and daily safety checks, with adjustments made as a result of these.
The effectiveness of the steps you take to promote children's good health and well being including those to prevent the spread of infection and those taken when children are ill	• In your routine do you allow time for rest? • Does your routine allow time for physical exercise for all children? • Do you have posters etc showing children hygiene routines such as hand washing or nose blowing? • How do you prevent the spread of illness and care for children who become ill whilst with you? • Do you have a named first aider and is this person responsible for checking the first aid kit regularly? The stock needs to be checked and signed. Do you use gloves when administering first aid?	Copies of routine showing time allowed for rest and exercise. Copies of routine posters. Witness statement from staff demonstrating support. Notices. Newsletters. Training log. First aid kit – with stocklist signed and dated. Prospectus with information relating to keeping healthy.

	• Do you wear coloured plasters on cuts when preparing food? • Do parents know that they are responsible for keeping you informed of their children's health issues e.g. contact with infectious disease? • Do you have a protocol of informing parents when there is an outbreak of infectious disease? • What do you do if a child tells you on arrival that they have been sick during the night? • Does your policy state that in case of sickness a child should not return for at least 48 hours? • Do you sterilise all feeding equipment and resources?	
	• Do you update children's medical history regularly? • Do you have spare clothing? • Do you dispose of nappies etc appropriately? • Do you ensure that any animals kept on the premises or visiting the premises do not pose a health risk? • Does your setting have good ventilation?	
How well you work in partnership with parents and others to safeguard children	• Do you offer informative advice to parents with children with infectious illnesses? • How do you consult with parents about issues relating to child protection? • How do you keep parents/carers informed? • Do staff have a working knowledge of what everyone needs to do? • Are records kept securely, confidentially and accurately?	
The staff's knowledge and understanding of child protection/safeguarding issues and procedures.	• Do you address the issue of safeguarding children in your staff induction procedures? • Do all staff receive training in safeguarding children is this updated regularly? State how regularly.	Attendance certificates from safeguarding children training. Copy of induction procedure. Copy of What to do if you suspect a child is being abused.

How effectively is the provision in the Early Years Foundation Stage led and managed?

Questions from pages 15,16 and 17 Ofsted SEF guidance.	Features to consider and reflective practice	Evidence suggestions
Suitable people • How well you ensure the suitability and qualifications of the adults looking after children or having unsupervised access to them. • How you identify the training needs of all adults working with children • How you organise training, is training cascaded to other staff	• Do you have a training matrix? • Is training offered to all staff on a need basis? • Do you use training cascade forms and have meetings where training is cascaded? • Do you consult your local early years training guide regularly? • Do you ensure that all staff can take part in qualification courses and long courses? • Are staff encouraged to take part in training and not put off by choosing between payrises and training opportunities.	Both training matrix and training cascade forms are in the back of this book. Copies of Criminal Record Bureau checks – dates and numbers – kept confidentially. Completed training matrix.
Suitable premises, environment and equipment • How effectively and efficiently you deploy resources: this includes any staff or assistants. • The quality and effectiveness of risk assessments and actions you take to manage or eliminate risks • How well you ensure trips/activities take place away from the premises are safe • How well you ensure all equipment is maintained to a safe and acceptable standard • How are the premises kept safe and secure so that children cannot leave alone or others gain unsupervised access.	• Are staff clear as to what their duties are on a daily basis? • Are staff aware of the need to ensure ratios are maintained at all times? • Are risk assessments and safety checks thorough? • Do you visit sites for outings beforehand to check their safety and suitability? • You need to get written parental consent to take children on outings. • High regard must be placed on ratios during outings, a ratio of 1 member of staff to every 2 children is recommended. • Do staff have clearly defined responsibilities during outings? • Do you take appropriate records with you on trips? • Do drivers have adequate insurance to take children on outings if cars are used? • Do coaches or any public transport that you use have adequate safety equipment? • Do you complete a full risk assessment annually? • Are all doors and gates locked and secured at all times that children are on the premises?	Staff rotas. Copies of safety checks, evaluated and actioned. Copies of annual risk assessments. Copy of visitors book- must have columns for name, time in, time out, purpose for visit,
Inclusion • How well you promote inclusive practice, including factors affecting all areas of learning and development so that all children have their welfare needs met and achieve as well as they can • How well you ensure Individual Educational Plans for children with specific identified needs are in place and kept up to date.	• Do you continually consider the needs of all children – those without additional needs also require their needs to be met? • Do you share these records on a need to know basis with other professionals? • Do you set aside time for all staff to be able to complete records?	Copies of training certificates. Copies of up to date Individual Education Plans.

Documentation		
• How well you maintain records, policies and procedures required for safe and efficient management of the EYFS and to ensure that the needs of all children are met	• Are policies updated regularly ie. annually? • Do staff and parents have the opportunity to contribute to policies?	Copies of policies.
Organisation		
• How effectively you strive for improvement to provide high quality care and education • How effectively you monitor provision and outcomes for children through regular quality checks and self assessment, and identify targets for further improvement • To what extent you are able to maintain continuous improvement, including improvements identified in any previous Ofsted inspection reports	• Are your improvements sustainable?	Do you have copies of financial analysis to prove that you can sustain improvements? Copies of previous Ofsted reports with actions taken.
Learning and development		
• How effectively you make use of data from observational assessment of children to help staff plan their support for children's learning and development regardless of background, gender, ethnicity, culture, learning difficulties and/or disabilities	• This relates to the unique child and meeting their individual needs using observations to inform planning.	
Partnership working		
• How well you work with parents, carers, other providers, services and employers and take into consideration ethnic background, home language, family background, religion/faith, learning difficulties and/or disabilities and gender to promote children's care and education	• Do you encourage parents of different cultures to come in to share aspects of their culture e.g. clothing, festivals, food?	

Section 6 – Put everything together from previous questions and tell Ofsted how good your setting is.

How well do you promote inclusive practice?	Features to consider/reflective practice	Evidence suggestions
How accessible is your building?	• Could a parent or child with mobility difficulties easily access the building.	Photos of access to building and invoices or quotations for improvements to be made?
How inclusive is your admissions policy? Are there any groups of children who may be excluded from your setting by your policy?	• Does you admissions policy explicitly explain a fair and non-discriminatory admissions criteria? • Do you bear in mind indirect discrimination and how the policy may be interpreted by all readers? • Are any children even unconsciously barred from attending your setting by outside influences e.g. faith of parents etc?	Copy of admissions policy. Witness statement from parent.
How effective and inclusive are your policies and procedures?	• Do you pay due regard to your policies and procedures in the day-to-day running of the setting? • Are policies and procedures reviewed regularly at least once a year? Do parents have the opportunity to be involved in the writing of policies?	Copies of policies and procedures. Look around your setting do you have children from a variety of ethnic backgrounds, do you have children with special needs? – If the answer is no can you explain why this might be? Is it because there are no such children in your community or is it because for some reason that you need to explore they are barred from attending your setting?
Are they available to and understood by all parents, staff and volunteers?	• Are policies displayed in a folder or on the notice board? • Do parents know that they have access to them?	Records of policy reviews including parental contributions.
Do you make them available in the languages of the children who attend?		Copies of policies that have been translated to different languages.
How well do you work in partnership with parents and others to meet every individual needs?	• Do you consider input from parents throughout the child's time at the setting? • Do you liaise effectively with other settings the child attends? • Do you involve other professionals e.g. portage workers?	Evidenced and recorded in child's records.
Do you consider boys and girls when planning activities?	• Boys are not less able than girls, though research has proven that they are achieving less well than girls. Do you consider boys' interests and learning styles in your planning? Do you allow for both passive learning and active learning in your planning?	It is no longer enough to say every activity is open to all children: you need to consider both the needs of boys – to be inquisitive, explorers, active and problem solvers and girls to use more language, story telling and creative activities.
How well do you meet the needs of children with learning difficulties and or disabilities and English as an additional language?		
How well do you ensure that your environment and resources are available to all children?	• Clearly labelled resources. • Clearly defined areas of learning. • Free-flow indoor and outdoor play.	
	• Resources and equipment that are of child height.	
How inclusive and welcoming is your service?	• Imagine what your setting is like for any parent or child visiting for the first time. • Posters reflecting positive images and community languages.	

How well do you maintain continuous improvement?	Features to consider/reflective practice	Evidence suggestions
What steps you take to evaluate your provision for children's learning and development.	• Reviews of learning environment and resources available. • Observations on a particular area or resource to see how children are using it. • How do you document children's work so that they can reflect on their achievements and progress?	
Who do you involve in your self evaluation process? Does it include children, parents, assistants, staff and volunteers?	• Do you observe children as part of your self evaluation by standing back to track children and check that your judgements are accurate? • Do you have a peer observation system? • Do you send questionnaires to parents and children to help evaluate your service? • Do you use the SEF to support continuous improvement in your setting? If so, how?	Photos of children's achievements. Refer to quality assurance awards – you don't have to write in detail but have information available on inspection. Plans. Copies of questionnaires and responses.
If your self evaluation gives a balanced view of the setting's strengths and areas for improvement.	• Do you take a balanced approach to self evaluation, remembering to celebrate achievements as well as identifying areas for improvement?	
If the action you take to tackle identified weaknesses, including those identified at the last inspection and monitoring visit from your development worker if applicable, is effective in terms of improved provision and outcomes for the children who attend	• Describe what action you have taken to tackle any identified weaknesses by outside agencies and how as a result your provision has improved.	Actions plans.
If your plans for the future are well targeted to bring about further improvement.	• Do you have realistic targets for the future that take into account your strengths and weaknesses, and barriers that you may meet along the way? • Do you have a vision and mission statement?	Copies of future plans.

How effective is your provision in meeting the needs of children in the Early Years Foundation Stage?	Features to consider/ reflective practice	Evidence suggestions
The needs of all children are routinely met through recognising the uniqueness of each child	• Using observations to inform planning	Even if you grade yourself as outstanding you need to consider what you would like to do better.
The setting supports every child so that no group or individual is disadvantaged		
All children make progress in their learning and development, children's welfare is promoted	• This is assessing the progress of each child through the development matters agenda. Knowing where the child is now and what the next steps are for that child. It is also about knowing the child's situation and things that may affect their wellbeing and development e.g. a family breakdown.	
Partnerships in the wider context are used to promote good quality education and care	• Do you liaise with other settings, other professionals, parents and your development worker to promote and improve the quality of care?	
The planning for improvement, including processes of self evaluation, is effective.	• This is about your self evaluation and planning for the future taking into account your strengths and weaknesses. It is about the opportunities that you may have and the barriers you may face in order to move forward and how you intend to overcome them. For example, you may plan to build an exciting new outside area, but a possible barrier would be lack of funds. Your way forward may be to engage parents in fundraising and building. This section also covers general action plans brought about through reflective practice.	

Part C – Information about compliance with statutory requirements.

To complete this section of the SEF you will need to refer to the Statutory Framework for the EYFS. You need the latest update- currently May 2008.

You need to judge yourself regarding the requirements as being Fully in place, Partly in place or Not in place. In most cases your judgement will need to be fully in place and in some instances you cannot operate if they are not in place.

Annex C on page 26 of the guidance to completing the SEF refers to what these definitions mean, however we feel that to be:

Fully in place you need to be confident and able to evidence that you are fully meeting the requirements.

Partly in place you need evidence of what you are doing to meet the requirements fully for example you need to show that you have booked on relevant courses or had invoices for work to be carried out.

Requirements that are judged by you not to be not in place will need to have a substantial reason why they are not met and a description of your intentions of meeting them.

Learning and development requirements	Aspects of specific welfare requirements	Evidence suggestions
LD 1 – The early learning goals – the knowledge skills and understanding that young children should have acquired by the end of the academic year in which they reach 5.	• Refer to pages 12- 16 of the statutory framework. This is about how you support children to progress through Development Matters towards the early learning goals.	Observations and assessment for each child during their time in the setting. They aren't expected to have attained the ELGs, but be working towards them.
LD 2 – The educational programmes – the development matters skills and processes that are required to be taught to young children	• Refer to pages 12 – 16 of the statutory framework. • This is about planning for continuous provision. It is about the balance of adult-led and child-initiated activities. It is about knowing what children need to learn throughout their time in the setting. This concerns in particular your long term planning. It is also about understanding child development and providing age stage appropriate activities and resources for each individual child.	Long, medium and short term plans.
LD3 – The assessment arrangements – the arrangements for assessing young children to ascertain their achievements	• Refer to pages 16 -18 of the statutory framework. • This is about assessments made through observations and the next steps to take linking these back to Development Matters.	Observations showing links to planning.

Welfare requirements - safeguarding and promoting children's welfare	Aspects of specific welfare requirements	Evidence suggestions
W1.1 The provider must take necessary steps to safeguard the welfare of children in the setting	• Refer to pages 22-25 of the statutory framework – this relates to safeguarding children (child protection), information, complaints, premises, security outings and equal opportunities. • Staff training • Incident sheets • Criminal Record Bureau (CRB) checks	Safeguarding policy and procedures. Guidance on what to do if you suspect a child is being abused flow charts. CRB checks. Copies of incident sheets.
W1.2 The provider must promote the good health of the children, take necessary steps to prevent the spread of infection and take appropriate action when they are ill	• Refer to pages 26 and 27 of the statutory framework. • This relates to medicines, illness and injuries, food and drink and smoking.	Copies of these policies. Administering medicine procedure. No smoking policy Incident and accident books.
W1.3 Children's behaviour must be managed effectively and in a manner appropriate for their stage of development and particular needs.	• Refer to page 28 of statutory framework. • This is about behaviour management – do you and all your staff understand the behaviour needs and expectations for various ages and stages of child development and the appropriate ways of responding to challenging behaviour at each stage?	This is now in your inclusion policy. Individual behaviour plans.

Welfare requirements - suitable people	Aspects of specific welfare requirements	Evidence suggestions
W2.1 Adults looking after children, or having unsupervised access to them, must be suitable to do so	• Refer to pages 29 – 30 of the statutory framework. • This is about the suitability of practitioners about safe recruitment. • Keeping records safely with due regard to confidentiality.	Copies of recruitment advertisements. Copies of interview format and questions. CRB checks Continued professional development.
W2.2 Adults looking after children must have appropriate qualifications, training, skills and knowledge	• Refer to page 31 of the statutory framework – this is self explanatory.	Copies of qualification certificates.
W2.3 Staffing arrangements must be organised to ensure safety and to meet the needs of the children	• Refer to page 32 of the statutory framework. • This is about deployment of staff.	

Welfare requirements – suitable premises, environment and equipment	Aspects of specific welfare requirements	Evidence suggestions
W3 Outdoor and indoor spaces, furniture equipment, and toys must be safe and suitable for their purpose.	• Refer to pages 33- 36 of the statutory framework • This is about risk assessments – these must clearly state when it was carried out, by whom, date of review and any action taken following review or incident. Ensuring that appropriate space is allocated for each child. Its about public liability insurance. • It is also about fire safety including fire procedures, fire detection and smoke detectors. Making sure toys are safe and from reputable providers. • It is about keeping records safely –with prior arrangement with Ofsted these may be kept off the premises.	Copies of fire drills and appropriate actions taken as a result of their evaluation.

Welfare requirements – suitable premises, environment and equipment	Aspects of specific welfare requirements	Evidence suggestions
W4 – Organisation Providers must plan and organise their systems to ensure that every child receives an enjoyable and challenging learning and development experience that is tailored to meet their individual needs	• Refer to page 37 of the statutory framework. • This is about ensuring that individual needs of children are met. • Its about assigning a key person to each child. It concerns ensuring that there is a balance of adult led and child initiated activities. • It is also about observations informing planning.	Your planning cycle. Reviews of the learning environment.

Welfare requirements – suitable premises, environment and equipment	Aspects of specific welfare requirements	Evidence suggestions
W5 Documentation and reporting. Providers must maintain records, policies and procedures required for the safe and efficient management of the settings and to meet the needs of the children	• Refer to pages 38 – 40 of the statutory framework. • This is about the data you have in place on each individual child • Information that needs to be submitted to the local education authority each year • How records and reviews and maintained. • Displaying registration certificate.	Copies of children's records safely kept.

You need to declare whether you are on the voluntary or compulsory part of the register - (mostly you will be compulsory i.e. caring for children from 0 – 8 years, whose provision is not exempt e.g. nannies) and the number of children that you are registered for.

First Impressions Count

As we all know first impressions really do count, we are genetically programmed in a way that means they have to. This is true even for your Ofsted inspector. The inspectors are professional people who aren't going to be fooled by the veneer of everything on the surface looking good but the practice being poor, and they aren't going to make judgements solely based on their first impressions, they are professionally far more objective than that, but the first impression does influence opinion and can change the feel of a visit. The following statement is taken directly from an Ofsted report: 'It is obvious from the moment the doors open and the children rush in that this is a happy and lively place where learning is fun.'

Before they arrive the inspector will have used their intuition to gauge what their expectations are and what they are going to find from reading your completed Self-Evaluation Form. This chapter aims to explore first impressions and how we can ensure that they are favourable in getting a true impression and judgement of your setting.

Hopefully the Ofsted inspector will have arrived at your door safely having been informed of how to gain access to your building. On her walk from the car or train to the door of your setting she is going to be looking around her to see if the setting is inviting and welcoming.

She is going to ring on your doorbell and may have to wait in the foyer for a few minutes, this can be an illuminating experience and one you should try yourself to give a true reflection of what it is going to be like for her. Ask yourself the questions: Is it warm, welcoming and comfortable? It's worth providing somewhere for parents and carers to sit. Does everyone in your foyer feel at ease and welcome? Are any information and notices given in an accessible manner to everyone, including those with additional needs? My experience of standing waiting in the foyer as a mother or as a visitor to a setting have not always been a positive experience and can colour my view of that setting.

As a visitor I often just stand and listen and wonder what it would be like to be a parent or child in that setting, especially a new parent – do I feel that I belong? Or is it a bit cliquey, are parents exchanging information which is sensitive and that really shouldn't be aired in public? Are they chatting about the setting in a positive and encouraging manner? Am I spoken to or am I ignored? Is there something for me to do whilst I wait or something informative for me to read? The foyer is a hazy area of responsibility but you need to try and create an area that reflects the rest of the setting and shouldn't be overlooked in the whole picture.

It leaves a bad impression if the inspector has to ask for the book to sign in so when they arrive please remember to ask them to sign in the visitors' book. The visitors' book must have a column for the name, date, time in and out, company and purpose of visit. Also don't forget to tell the inspector about your emergency procedures and if there are any emergency drills planned for that day.

Be sure to open up on time everyday – if the inspector is waiting outside and you're late in opening the doors parents may start to grumble and it looks unprofessional and unorganised. It's a shame really that you may not receive brownie points for opening smack on time but you're sure to lose them for opening late! This may mean that you need to consider changing your practice to facilitate everything being ready and safe for the children to come in on time. If you have to put everything out each morning timing can be an issue especially if your staff are made up largely of parents who themselves need to drop children off at school. Can you think of ways to overcome this problem? If you have some staff who have no other commitments before sessions begin they could be paid to come in a little earlier with the sole purpose of setting up. This does need to be transparent to all staff or tension can build up within the team.

The greeting – this can be a tricky one! You're about to be inspected – you're bound to be anxious and possibly

more than a little tense - this is true for the whole team – but do try to relax, breathe deeply, be friendly and above all be professional! Find the time please to introduce the inspector to the whole team including any committee members who are present. Do show her where she can put her bag and coat and where the toilets are. It is likely to be whoever is on the door that day that welcomes the Ofsted Inspector so this could be the newest and least-trained member of staff. It is worth considering putting something in the staff induction programme that includes role-play situations. If the inspector arrives at the start of the session when the door is busy, how does the person on the door welcome them, manage to stay on the door and also inform the rest of the team that they are there? The solution to these types of problem will be different in every setting and needs to be discussed and tried out using various scenarios during training days.

Try to ensure that the dynamics of your team remain professional on inspection day. To witness the team working together in a friendly manner with good rapport will prove to the inspector that you work well together and will be supportive as a team during challenging times. Indicators of good team work are shared goals, respect and friendliness to one another. This is not about being matey it is about being professional and sincere in your approach to your work. The inspector will be experienced in what effective teamwork looks like, below are some indicators of positive teamwork.

+ Does the room appear organised?

+ Are the staff communicating verbally, is there also evidence of non-verbal communication e.g. message books?

+ Are the children happy and on task, and are their physical needs being met?

+ Do the staff appear to be aware of their roles and responsibilities?

+ Is there a happy and positive atmosphere?

+ Are the displays up-to-date?

+ Is the routine displayed and followed?

+ Do the children respond to the adults?

+ Do the adults respond to the children?

Your approach to the children in the setting must also reflect normality – try to be the same with the children as you always are, any tension that you're feeling will rub off on them. It is so easy to detect false behaviour – the children will be the first to see through it! You're not going to get an inadequate judgement if on the day the inspector comes six children are crying, Jonnie and Alice have just bitten each other, the school fish has died and a member of staff has PMT. Unless of course you leave the six children uncomforted, you don't help Jonnie and Alice to resolve their dispute amicably, you leave the fish floating in the bowl and you let the member of staff wreak havoc! Its how you handle the situations you're faced with that count as well as what caused them in the first place, could reflective practice have identified areas for improvement that would negate these problems? For example, have observations revealed that children are unsettled on arrival and have you and your team discussed ways to improve this situation e.g. by moving straight into free-flow play at the beginning of a session.

It is important that all staff are identifiable, this is for children and parents and carers on an everyday level, as well as for inspectors. You can achieve this simply and relatively cheaply by giving them all name badges to wear, or tabards or the same bright coloured tee-shirts. A named photograph displayed with staff titles, responsibilities and training is also a nice touch. Not only does being identifiable help everyone know who everyone else is, it also demonstrates a sense of pride in your place of work.

Once the inspector has walked in the door and been greeted and signed in she will no doubt pause and look around the room to get a feel for the place, to get an idea of the general ambiance: this is another chance to make a positive first impression. They will want to see a bright, airy and clean room, that doesn't mean there is no paint or water or sand or glitter, those things are meant to be there. It means that there aren't five year-old cobwebs and displays of children's work that are so old that the paper is curled and the season has passed.

We all have our own ideas of what's important to us and the Ofsted inspector is no different: there will be something that she is extra keen on to look at first. However, during the course of the visit she will look at everything that she wants to. Some of the things that leave a lasting impression from first glance are listed on the check list at the end of this section.

A good way to know what the first impression your setting may give is to try to experience it yourself, or visit other settings to see how their practice is similar or varies from yours and to identify your own strengths and weaknesses and see where improvements can be made. You could set up a video to record the beginning of your sessions or simply video around the setting – it is amazing what you will see through this. Or get a fresh pair of eyes in to look for you, it might be worth asking your local early years team if they could evaluate some areas for you to provide reassurance. You should network with other local settings and within the team as you may get ideas that you could use. Peer observations with feedback and evaluation at staff meetings will help you to identify areas of strength both individually and as a team and identify those areas that require development – there is more information on these in the Preparing for your inspection chapter of this book.

As stated at the beginning of this chapter we all know that first impressions count but they can be misguided, I'm sure we've all formed impressions in the past only to be proven wrong so it doesn't all hang on first impressions, it is more about good practice which will become evident during the visit. But if things start off badly and the inspector's view is tainted it can prove to be a long haul to get things back on track.

First Impressions Checklist

What the inspector may look for	Comment	Met	Partly Met	Not Met
Is there a range and variety of activities available that are age or stage appropriate?	Are you sure that activities suit all children in the setting – e.g. no small parts?			
Are activities set out on different levels?	Are there table-top, floor, wall activities?			
Do activities encourage exploration and investigation?	Do adults model investigation and exploration?			
Are resources up to date and relevant?	Children need to experience activities relevant to their lives			
Are all resources fit for purpose?	All pieces present for puzzles, no splinters on wood, all pages of books			
Is the paint fresh?	Is paint stirred and refreshed daily – are there plenty of colours for children to mix			
Is the playdough fresh?	Do the children make the playdough themselves, is there a choice of colour, texture and tools etc			
Can children initiate their own play through free choice?	This will be apparent immediately			
Are resources clearly labelled with words and pictures?	Children first learn to read through looking at pictures and identifying symbols and making representations			
Are all the staff interacting and engaging with the children?	This can include observing the children			
Is there a clear learning intention to each activity?	Would every adult present know what you are hoping to get from each activity?			
Are the activities provided exciting?	Ask yourself 'Would I want to play here if I was a child?			
Do the children appear to be happy and engaged?	If children are bored they can become frustrated			
Do children and adults appear to have a sense of pride in this setting?				
Are there displays of children's work: are these clearly labelled perhaps with a child's photo?	Is every child's work included? Are these up-to-date? Is all the work displayed the children's own or is it done by adults?			
Are displays child height?	Are they bright and colourful			
Would all children feel that they belong here?	Does each child have their own peg, tray etc			
Are staff easily identifiable?	Do the staff wear uniforms or name badges?			
If English was not my first language could I access information?	Consider how you make sure that messages are received and understood?			
Is there a visual timetable?	This helps children with routine and transitions			
Is there access to plenty of malleable materials?	There should be around five malleable activities available in a pre-school setting			
Do children know who their key person is?	Have you got key person lists with photographs of the key persons?			
Are areas of learning easily identifiable?	Do children and adults know where to go to do each activity?			
Does the setting smell fresh?	This is especially important in settings used by others and if there are stale food smells			

What the inspector may look for	Comment	Met	Partly Met	Not Met
Do children have free access to drinking water?	Ideally, free-flowing water, but be sure its fresh daily			
Are the toilets well stocked with soap, handtowels and toilet paper etc?	It is best practice to use squeezable bottle soap not bars of soap.			
Is there access to natural materials?	It is good to have natural resources both indoors and outdoors			
Are all cultures equally reflected?	This is especially important where some cultures are not physically present			
Is there free-flow play indoors and outdoors?	Are staff actively encouraging free-flow play?			
Are all staff well deployed?	Does every member of staff know what they are doing and why they are doing it?			

Preparing for Inspection

As we reflect more and more on our practice, less and less specific preparation will be required for an Ofsted inspection as the idea is that we'll always be ready. When considering preparation for an Ofsted inspection we're not talking about the stereotypical image of the caretaker painting the walls two minutes before the inspector is due to arrive. In this chapter we are looking more broadly at what practitioners need to do to prepare for inspection, both physically and mentally, because it can't just be pulled out of the bag on the day. A knock on the door by the Ofsted inspector should be a welcome visit that isn't going to phase any of the practitioners in the setting because they are all prepared and equipped with the knowledge understanding and strategies to cope.

In preparation for inspection you need to ensure that your SEF is completed

competently, accurately and that it is up to date. It isn't compulsory but it is strongly recommended that you have it filled in. Not having done so could adversely effect the outcome of the inspection so don't procrastinate, guidance is given in this book to help you complete it. If you haven't completed the form before the inspection you may be asked to do it on the day and this can cause anxiety and in the rush you could miss vital points, it simply isn't possible to fill it in properly under these conditions. Make sure that you have a hard copy on hand for yourself to refer to during the inspection.

As you update your SEF be certain to send the updates to Ofsted – this is easy to do online – so that they always have current and relevant information. The inspector will read your SEF before visiting your setting so its important that it is up to date – in fact the online version of the SEF may be frozen approximately two days before the inspection giving you clear indication that you are about to be inspected – but this is NOT a guarantee.

When anticipating starting the SEF you need to be organised and share the task of completing it between the entire staff team. Effective team work is an essential component in any setting. Without effective team work, a setting cannot function properly and maintain standards. The inspector will be very experienced in looking for and identifying signs that show team work is either effective or ineffective in the setting. The sense of teamwork in a setting reflects the culture and ethos. Leaders and managers in settings can use the following checklist to help gain an insight into the sense of teamwork established in different rooms and/or the setting as a whole.

My Inspection Case Study

In January 2009 we were inspected by Ofsted. We had not completed the SEF – It had been started but I was put off by about page three! The Ofsted Inspector questioned me as to why it hadn't been completed and I explained that there had been other priorities, for example writing new policies in line with the EYFS. In place of the SEF, the inspector gave me a list of questions to be completed during her inspection. This put me under intense pressure and I feel my responses didn't offer a true reflection of the setting. I think if we had been any further into the implementation of the EYFS that the inspector would have been less understanding to the SEF not being completed. At the time of writing I do not have any outcome of my inspection.

Pre-School Leader

My Inspection Case Study

As a team completing our SEF we discussed and realised that while we were always careful to be aware of and incorporate parents' and carers' wishes into our routine that we actually didn't very often ask children for their opinions. When we thought about this even more and discussed this with our quality improvement mentor from early years we realised that we could offer children far greater opportunities for choice throughout the session. The SEF encouraged us to think more deeply about our practice and make improvements that have had a directly positive impact on the children in our care.

Pre-School Leader

The Ofsted inspector will probably take points from the SEF to concentrate on during the visit – although this won't necessarily be the entire focus of the visit – but it does mean that information needs to be accurate and an honest reflection – this is no time for modesty! It is also a time to think of moving your practice forward in a positive way and not seeing problems as obstacles or barriers to improvement but as challenges to overcome. But don't panic nothing is perfect straight away and the inspector is not looking for perfection but looking that you are moving forwards and trying to improve all the time. Even if you judge yourself to be outstanding she will want to see how you intend to improve even further. A positive outcome of having an accurately completed SEF could be that the inspector may not check out everything that you do and it may shorten the inspection. Not only do you need to complete your SEF but also get to know your SEF: be aware of, and have a working knowledge of, what actions are being taken, exactly what progress has been made, where your strengths are and where more work is required. It is important that the whole team is involved in this and not just the person responsible for completing the SEF.

If your setting is taking part in any kind of quality assurance award it is useful to have the relevant information for that to hand also. Ofsted will be interested to see any completed or current modules with development plans and evidence of the impact these schemes have had on your practice and experiences for the children within the setting. If you have any certificates or plaques for quality assurance awards or training these need to be displayed as they evidence continued professional development and good practice.

Now we need to think of the more practical things. Can the inspectors find your setting easily? Is the address and phone number up-to-date with Ofsted and are postcodes accurate for your building? This is especially important if the inspectors are using a satellite navigation system to find you.

If you are a pre-school or day care setting are you clearly advertised and signposted? Is car parking convenient and easy to find? If the answer to these two questions is no, is there anything that you can do about it? There is nothing more stress-inducing than not being able to find your way somewhere then not being able to park the car, not having the right

change for the meter and then having a long walk laden down with bags – you really don't want your inspector to arrive to inspect you under these sorts of conditions. It may be that all you can do is inform them before the visit where they will need to park and if they will need money and how much etc.

Consider the access to your building; this needs to be easy to use for all people including those with additional needs. Can the inspector find where to get in? Is there an efficient way of the door being answered at all times including before the session begins?

With every action that you take it is important to always ensure that the children are at the heart of all that happens. You need to ask yourself how you put children at the centre of your practice and be able to demonstrate this to the inspector. So, for example if through peer observations you decided that your welcome was poor and you decided to change it, you need to put the child at the heart and think 'what would make this a better experience for all the children?' The next step is to involve the children and their parents and carers by asking for their opinions and valuing them, in this way they will then be far more supportive in implementing any change. Through peer observation you may realise that a particular member of staff does something especially well and may therefore decide to all use that method of practice throughout the setting.

At all times you need to ensure that your environment is safe and stimulating for children to learn and develop and to make any changes that are necessary. Use the skills you have learnt during reflective practice to assess this, asking yourself relevant questions such as are there defined areas of learning? Is it bright and airy? Am I an effective practitioner setting activities up in an inviting manner? Be aware that you need to have robust systems in place for risk assessments, equipment maintenance and safety checks.

It is vital to read through your last inspection as a whole team to address any outstanding issues and simply to remind yourselves of its content. Try not to take the previous report too personally or as criticism, if you can look at it more in terms of guidance for improvement you are more likely

to have an open mind when making those improvements. Just because this is Ofsted it doesn't mean that the judgements are always right, so you need to consider them carefully and dispassionately and then act accordingly. It is vitally important that you have completed any actions from the previous Ofsted inspection, but if you haven't then you need to be able to justify why this is the case. When you look at the last report it is also a good time to reflect on all the improvements that you have made, however sometimes in the rush to improve certain areas it is easy to lose sight of the good you were already doing so this is a good time to make sure you haven't let some areas of good practice slide.

Your polices need to be always up-to-date, reviewed and in order. Best practice is to ensure that these are read and signed by each member of staff and committee members as proof that they have read them. It is also good to have enabled staff to contribute to policies in order to give them a sense of ownership. This can of course be a lengthy process, but you could consider one or two policies a month over the course of an academic year. Guidance on writing policies and the requirements of individual policies can be got from your local Early Years and Childcare Service or from the Pre School Learning Alliance. Of course all policies are important but some details are more vital so pay particular attention that everyone is aware of the safeguarding children policy and those relating to staff conduct. It's also important that parents are aware of policies and are able to access them – could you include a policy of the month on your newsletters for example to ensure staff and parents have a working knowledge of practice policies?

Be sure that your planning is up to date – its good for it to be annotated with changes made in response to children, that's exactly what the inspectors will want to see but make sure this can be evidenced in your observations.

Talk to the staff – staff are likely to be anxious of inspections particularly if this is their first one or if they have had a bad experience of being inspected. Its best for staff to be prepared, so brief them with likely scenarios and empower them with responses. The inspector will speak to all staff members so it is important to help them to understand the way questions may be posed and the jargon that may be used. However, most important is to reassure staff of your faith in them and of their good practice so that they can relax and are able to perform to their best ability. This can be achieved through in-house training, constant communication via staff meetings, making sure all staff have access to and are supported during training so that they are well informed and knowledgeable on all aspects of their role.

Have you got an operational plan or a wish list? If so consult it in preparation for inspection – are there any wishes that you could grant yourself? The feel-good factor of saying we've been able to develop our outdoor play recently by buying x, y or z is worth its weight in gold.

Are you part of a quality assurance scheme? Ofsted suggest that being part of such a scheme is not a guarantee of a good outcome but it is likely to have improved your practice in response to its questions and completed modules are helpful evidence for the inspector. It is estimated that somewhere in the region of 85% of pre-school settings on a quality assurance scheme receive outstanding Ofsted judgements (www. ofsted.gov.uk 02.02.09).

Ofsted will consider your partnership with parents so in preparation it is important that you do this too. Try to think of imaginative ways of sharing information with all parents and enhancing the relationship so that parents are not only informed but are able to become engaged in the setting – it is proven that parents involved in this early stage of their child's education will be more likely to stay involved in later stages of their education.

Something that is often overlooked in preparation for an inspection is whether your setting is culturally aware, an excuse often proffered for not being is that 'we don't have any children from that culture here' – however it is even more important to reflect all members of a society for children who aren't going to have personal experiences of them so that they don't form prejudices and stereotypical viewpoints. Your inclusion practices are the golden thread that you will notice run through all of the SEF questions, therefore it is something to consider extremely carefully and to be transparent about.

Continued professional development is a phrase on all of our minds. Make sure you are aware of all staff training needs and training undertaken according to need. For this you

may need a training matrix which is included in this book. You will want to have a system in place whereby training is cascaded perhaps during staff meetings, or by a simple form that staff fill in when they have been on courses saying what they learnt and how it effected their practice – this can be displayed on the staff notice board for all to read, again a cascade form is included in this book.

This chapter links closely with the chapter on first impressions and it would be wise to go through that to make sure you have everything in place, we've talked a lot about implementing change but guard against making change for the sake of it, if something is good and working well then leave it alone and give yourselves a pat on the back. It is just as important for the whole team to celebrate good practice and achievements as it is to be aware of areas in need of improvement.

Opposite is an example form of how to record any training undertaken by staff, and below a suggested training matrix to track at a glance the qualifications and training of all staff.

Cascade from training

Title of course attended	
Date of course attended	
Names of staff attending course	
General description of content of course	
Three points for development from course or ideas gained from course	1. 2. 3.
On a scale of 1 to 10 how effective was the course in meeting your requirements (1 being lowest and 10 being highest) circle as appropriate then explain your answer.	1 2 3 4 5 6 7 8 9 10

PHOTOCOPIABLE FORMS

Training matrix

Staff Name	Qualification and date gained	CRB – Date and number	Ist Aid – date	Appraisal – date	Safe guarding children – date	Supervision – date	Courses requested – identified at appraisal and supervision	Courses attended – and date	Cascade – yes/no – and date

The Inspection Day

So the inspector has arrived, what should you do? The most important thing is to carry on as normal, once you've got over the first feelings of 'they're here'! Carrying on and treating it as a normal day ensures stability for the children and that you will be showing yourselves at your best to the inspector. What you don't want is the inspector to hear a member of staff saying to you or someone else "why are you doing that?" implying that what is happening is not normal practice.

Be as accommodating as possible, remember the inspector will have a laptop with them to record their observations and findings, and therefore will need space in each room. It is probably worth mentioning at this point that the inspector is not there to look for negatives, but will be looking to see how you demonstrate that the Early Years Foundation Stage is in practice in your setting.

Your staff team will need support and may well be feeling particularly nervous. It is important they feel reassured, particularly after being asked questions by the inspector.

How to support your staff team during an inspection:

You'll know your team, so you'll know who will be unfazed by the inspector arriving and who will be panicking.

To alleviate the panicking you just need to carry on as normal and give reassurance as necessary.

Introduce members of staff confidently to the inspector and mention their role in the setting and level of qualification as well as their name.

Make sure as well the kettle is always ready to boil, there are plenty of clean mugs and milk ready for staff during their breaks.

What about if you have doubts about your inspector?

It is very unlikely that this would happen, but there are few steps to follow if this should occur:

Talk to another senior member of staff to see if they have doubts as well.

Your doubts might be about general awareness, competency, conduct and level of professionalism.

If you feel you do have cause for concern and that the inspection judgment might be compromised, you should talk to the inspector, so the situation can hopefully be resolved there and then. If you are not happy with the outcome of this conversation, you should phone Ofsted on 08456 404040. Formal complaints can be made at any stage during the inspection or up to thirty calendar days from the date of publication of any report.

So the inspection is over and you're about to receive your feedback, remember the following:

+ Take a couple of deep breaths to calm your nerves.

+ Make sure you go somewhere quiet for the feedback, and ensure staff know not to interrupt you.

+ Listen carefully.

+ Jot down key points.

+ Ask questions to help your understanding and to clarify points.

+ If you're unclear about something ask for specific examples to help understanding.

+ Acknowledge the feedback.

+ Try not to focus just on any negatives but remember the positives as well and see the negatives as points for developing and improving practice.

+ Take time to sort out in your head what has been said before feeding back to the rest of the staff team.

Remember feedback is two way and if you feel you have justification to challenge something that has been said then do so clearly, concisely and with evidence which can be verbally explained. If you do this then at least when the inspector has gone you won't feel like you did nothing.

Unless the outcome of the inspection was inadequate or you have been given a time limit on certain points for action, give yourself a few days grace to digest all that has been said. Having given yourself this time, you will then be in a better position to take action on the points raised and identifying how to move forward with your practice.

My Inspection Case Study

During our inspection we found that the inspector went round talking to all members of staff and asking them about the nursery ethos and what was included in our SEF. As the whole staff team had been involved with the SEF, despite being nervous they were all able to explain their understanding of the SEF to the inspector.

Nursery Manager

Your Ofsted Grading

GRADE	WHAT IT MEANS	WHAT YOU MIGHT DO
Grade 1 OUTSTANDING	This applies to exceptional provision which is way above the norm. The standard of care is exemplary. It is highly effective at making sure that children make significant progress towards the early learning goals given their starting points. Overall, the practice is worth disseminating beyond the setting. Inspectors make very few recommendations to bring about minor improvements.	You might disseminate your practice by sharing your success with the parents, local community, local press and the sharing of practice at early years training sessions.
Grade 2 GOOD	This applies to strong provision in which children are well cared for. It is successful at making sure that children make good progress towards the early learning goals – given their starting points. Overall, the practice is worth reinforcing and developing. Inspectors will make recommendations for further improvement. Inspectors may raise actions to ensure that specific welfare requirements of the EYFS are met.	Reinforce the good practice and look to develop action plans to help continual development and maintain standards.
Grade 3 SATISFACTORY	This applies to provision which is sound but could do better. The standard of care is acceptable. Children's progress towards the early learning goals is steady, but slow given their starting points. Overall, the practice has scope for improvement. Inspectors will make recommendations for further improvement. Inspectors may raise action points to ensure that specific welfare requirements of the EYFS are met.	Read the report carefully to identify what needs to be changed. Prioritise realistic goals, take a step-by-step approach and don't try too much at once. To boost confidence ensure you consolidate good practice. Ask your local authority early years advisers for help and support.
Grade 4 INADEQUATE CATEGORY 1	This applies to provision which is weak. The standard of care is not good enough: one or more of the learning and development or general welfare requirements of the EYFS are not being met. Children make too little progress towards the early learning goals – given their starting points. There has been too little improvement since the last inspection. Overall, the quality of the provision gives cause for concern but is likely to improve without external help and support. You will receive a letter from Ofsted setting out the actions that must be taken and by what date, to remedy significant weaknesses. The registered person must notify Ofsted when the necessary action has been taken.	You should receive intervention from your local authority early years service to give help and guidance on implementing the action points outlined by Ofsted.
Grade 4 INADEQUATE CATEGORY 2	This applies to poor provision which needs urgent attention. The standard of care and/or early education is unacceptable. One or more of the learning and development or general welfare requirements of the EYFS are not being met. Children are not safeguarded and/or make little or no progress towards the early learning goals. There has been too little improvement since our last inspection. Overall, the quality of the provision gives cause for concern and is unlikely to improve without enforcement action being taken by us, and help and support from external agencies. Ofsted will take enforcement action and may issue a welfare requirements notice which sets out what welfare requirements are not being met, and what must be done to improve the provision, and by when.	You will receive further visits from Ofsted and will receive support from your local authority early years service.

After The Inspection

Your inspection is over, so what should you do apart from breathe a huge sigh of relief? First and most importantly celebrate the success of the inspection and identified areas of strength. This should involve every member of staff, as they will have all contributed to the outcome. Make sure you tell the parents and carers of the children in your setting and why not generate some positive publicity by contacting your local paper?

Once the euphoria and sense of relief is over, you will need to sit down quietly without any distractions and read the report and identify what is being said. Regardless of the grading outcome of the inspection, there will be changes that you should implement as part of the setting's continual development. This includes settings with an outstanding grading.

This might be particularly difficult if your inspection didn't go well or you were unhappy with the outcome. Your first impulse reaction might be to blame Ofsted, to blame yourself or another member of staff. It may take a while to be able to look at action points and outcomes with the perspective required. It is essential you reach the point of objectivity to be able to move forward. Don't blame anyone, including yourself, instead work on moving forward.

Part of moving forward is bound to involve change. By nature we are resistant to change so managers and leaders in settings need to look carefully at how they implement this change.

To begin it might be useful to answer questions in the box below to help gain an insight into the experience and impact of change.

Effects of change questionnaire

Think of any changes you have experienced.

How did you feel?

How would you have preferred to experience the change (if negative) OR what made the change successful (if positive)?

Why do you think someone introduced the change in the first place?

Was it what you wanted or needed?

Should your opinions count? Why?

When a change is planned or introduced the first thing that people ask themselves is how will this change affect me? This is particularly relevant if the change is presented to them with no discussion or explanation.

Change that is to be implemented after an inspection concerns everyone and therefore should involve everyone. This is essential if the change is going to be implemented successfully and have a positive impact on the setting. Even if the only involvement is being part of a discussion about how to move forward and work to implement action points.

For people to be accepting of change you need to be able to answer how the change will affect them as well as involve them to some degree in the planning of the change. This involvement helps to ensure that the change is implemented successfully and that the action points become part of practice.

Reasons for resistance to change

A desire not to loose something of value

A misunderstanding of the change and its implications

A belief that is doesn't make sense

A low tolerance for change - fear of not being able to develop new skills and behaviour required of them

Managing successful change

Keep the lines of communication open

If you can consult with the team do

Be prepared to listen to concerns and respond appropriately

Give explanations and reasons

Ensure the team know the benefits and implications of the change and specifically how it affects their job role?

Be honest about the expected affect of change

Review the affect of change after implementation

To implement the change effectively and monitor the process of implementation and the outcome, you need to set Specific, Measurable, Achievable, Realistic and Time-bound (SMART) targets and devise an action plan, as discussed in the chapter on reflective practice.

Moving forward after an inspection is essential, the temptation will be to sit back and think 'oh we don't need to worry about that for another 3 years.' For any development of practice and skills to become embedded in the day-to-day you need to start as soon as possible. This will then help to ensure you reap the benefits at your next inspection. Not only that though, it means you providing the best possible early years experience for the children who attend your setting.

Remember to inform Ofsted if.......

There is a change of leader/person in charge in your setting, even if this is only temporary e.g. maternity leave.

If a child or member of staff has a serious accident.

If a child or member of staff has a communicable illness.

If you wish to change the terms of your registration e.g. increase the number of children you care for.

Additionally, if you are a childminder, inform Ofsted if...

A person in your household turns 16.

You employ an assistant.

An adult moves in or out of your house..

You wish to build an extension to your house.

It is essential to inform Ofsted of any of the above, as failure to do so is likely to impact on the outcome of an inspection.

My Inspection Case Study

Our Ofsted inspection went well, we were graded outstanding. The inspector suggested we should look at developing our outside area. Through staff discussion we have written actions plans to extend our home corner provision outside by introducing garden furniture, a 'barbecue' and washing line with pegs. We are also going to create a minibeast area with lots of small logs on the ground and we are going to increase the children's digging area.

Early Years Advisor

Further Resources

Publications

Confident, Capable and Creative: Supporting Boys' Achievements (DCSF 2007)

Inclusion Development Programme: Supporting Children with Speech, Language and Communication Needs - Guidance for Practitioners in the Early Years Foundation Stage (DCSF 2008)

Key Elements of Effective Practice (KEEP) (DFES 2005)

Protection, Safety and Welfare in the Early Years (Practical Pre-School Books 2008)

Social and Emotional Aspects of Development: Guidance for Practitioners Working in the Early Years Foundation Stage (DCSF 2008)

Supporting Children Learning English as an Additional Language (DCSF 2007)

The Criminal Records Bureau Code of Practice and Explanatory Guide

The Data Protection Act

The Disability Discrimination Act

The Early Years Foundation Stage in Practice (Practical Pre-School Books 2009)

The Vetting and Barring Scheme (Independent Safeguarding Authority 2009)

Websites

www.cwdcouncil.org.uk

www.everychildmatters.gov.uk

www.ofsted.gov.uk

www.qca.org.uk

www.standards.dcsf.gov.uk/eyfs

www.standards.dcsf.gov.uk/nationalstrategies